CRAFTS FOR ALL SEASONS

Crafts for All Seasons

Shilpa Tulsian

New Age Publishers Pvt. Ltd
LONDON
DELHI KOLKATA PUNE HYDERABAD ERNAKULAM

REGD. OFFICE

8/1 Chintamoni Das Lane, Kolkata 700 009, India
email: ncbapvtltd@eth.net

OVERSEAS

NCBA (UK) Ltd, 149 Park Avenue North, Northampton, NN3 2HY, UK

EXPORT

NCBA Exports Pvt. Ltd, 212 Shahpur Jat, New Delhi 110 049
email: ncbaexp@ncbapvtltd.com

BRANCHES

208B Peacock Lane, Shahpur Jat
New Delhi 110 049
email: ncbadel@ncbapvtltd.com

House No. 3-1-315, 1st Floor
Nimboliadda, Kachiguda, **Hyderabad** 500 027
email: ncbahydb@ncbapvtltd.com

Shop Nos. 3 & 4, Vinayak Towers
681/B Budhwar Peth, Appa Balwant Chowk
Pune 411 002
email: ncbapune@ncbapvtltd.com

GSS Shopping Complex, 1st Floor
Opposite College Post Office, Convent Road
Ernakulam 682 035
email: ncbaernk@ncbapvtltd.com

CRAFTS FOR ALL SEASONS

First Published: 2011

PUBLISHER

New Age Publishers (P) Ltd
8/1 Chintamoni Das Lane, Kolkata 700 009

PRINTER

New Central Book Agency (P) Ltd
Web-Offset Division, Dhulagarh, Sankrail, Howrah

ISBN: 81-7819-078-8

Price: ₹ 350.00

Introduction

I have always gifted my family and friends handmade cards on their birthdays and anniversaries. They have appreciated my work and many of them wanted to learn this art. This inspired me to write this book which could be useful for making handmade gifts for all occasions.

This is a book for all craft lovers who need guidance in making handmade gifts and bring a glint of happiness in the eyes of their loved ones.

The handmade cards are easy to create and stunning to look at. These cards are always preserved because of the feelings attached with them. The beautifully decorated bags easily become the centre of attraction with their personalised look. Making these bags consume very little time and material. The chapter on gift hampers contains loads of fascinating ideas for decorating baskets as well. One can prepare these baskets well in advance and just fill with the goodies on the special day.

I have also included quotes for various occasions which can be used for writing the wishes on handmade cards. So whenever there is a special event coming up, just use any of the ideas from this book and make your gift memorable.

Acknowledgement

I thank the Almighty God for the ability that he has bestowed upon me. Without his divine grace this book would never have been possible.

I would like to thank my mother-in-law who stood by me throughout this project. My husband Atul was my constant source of strength. My loving children Devesh and Mahek were very cooperative whenever I was busy with my creative work.

I heartily thank my parents who believed my dream and stood by me with their love, support and encouragement. I thank my mother for her suggestions and creative ideas and my father for his moral support.

I thank my friend Kanchan Kabra for her guidance at every step of the book.

I dedicate this book to my father-in-law who taught me the value of time and hard work. His blessings will always give me the strength to accomplish my work.

CONTENTS

Crafts for All Seasons

Birthday Greeting Card

A simple birthday card which can be made with a few paper sheets. Quick and easy for giving that special feel!

You will need

Coloured chart paper 22cms X 36cms
Textured paper
Satin ribbons, Decorative flowers
Butterflies, silver glitter tube
Double sided tape, glue gun
Floral lace, stones, pips

1. Fold the coloured chart paper into half. Cut two rectangles of size 8cms X 11cms and 11cms X 11cms. Paste them on the card.

2. Paste a small size coloured sheet on the first rectangle. Arrange a few flowers, stones, pips on it.

3. Cut three small squares of size 4cms X 4cms of different colours. Stick them on the bigger square using double sided tape.

4. Stick satin ribbons to give the effect of gift boxes. Beautify with a floral lace and silver glitter.

Birthday Card Using Clay

A funny bunny rabbit moulded out of soft clay. This card can be gifted to younger children who would be delighted to display it on their board.

You will need

Chart paper 30cms X 22cms
Soft clay—Pink, White, Red, Blue, Green, Yellow
Thermocol pieces
Wrapping papers
Water colours, Glue
Silver glitter tube
Silver sequins

1. Using clay make all body parts of the rabbit.

2. Paste all these parts using gum.

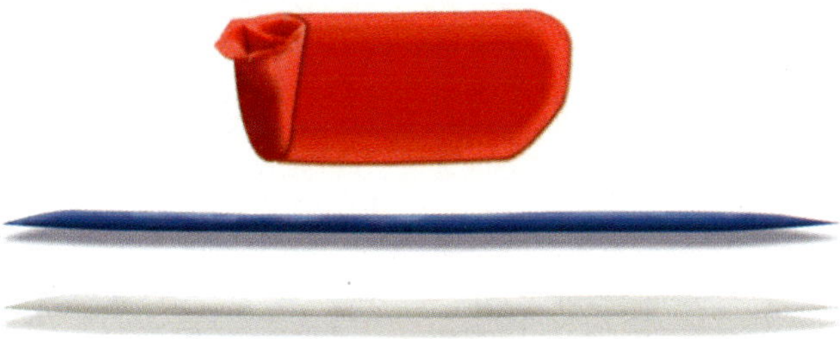

3. Make a thin strip of clay and roll it like a rose.
Make similar roses and arrange it like a bouquet.
Make two thin pipes of blue and white clay and
twist them together to make one pipe.

4. Wrap small squares and rectangular pieces of thermocol with different coloured wrapping papers and paste on the card. Paste the bunny rabbit on top of the gift box heap.

5. Paste the twisted clay pipes and the extra roses. Using water colours give shaded effect on the background and decorate with sequins and silver glitter.

50th Birthday Greeting Card

Finding a gift for somebody's 50th birthday is difficult. But a handmade card would always be appreciated.

You will need

Black, White, Golden chart paper
Golden tissue lace, golden rings, leaves
Golden ribbon, black satin ribbon
Printed or painted scenery 10cms X 20cms
Golden corrugated sheet
Golden, silver glitter
Thermocol sheet
Double sided foam tape (1.5mm thickness)
Glue, glue gun

1. Cut the thermocol sheet of size 30cms X 40cms. Cut black chart paper of the same size and paste on the thermocol. Keep it pressed under a heavy object for sometime. Cut the golden chart paper of size 22cms X 24cms, fold into half and paste it in the centre of the thermocol sheet.

2. Paste the scenery on the golden card and border with black satin ribbon. Paste the golden tissue lace on both the sides of the card. Stick golden rings, leaves and give grassy effect using golden glitter.

3. On the golden chart paper cut 5 and 0 (refer template) and outline with silver glitter. Using double tape stick on the left corner.

4. Paste the golden ribbons and decorate with silver glitter.

Birthday Greeting Card

This is a birthday card for all ages. Even for a 50th birthday this card would be appropriate.

You will need

Maroon chart paper size 36cms X 54cms
Golden chart paper size 25cms X 17cms
Golden tissue size 27cms X 15cms
Golden rings, sequins
Silver flowers, leaves
Golden, silver glitter
Gum, glue gun

1. Fold the maroon chart paper in half. Paste the golden chart paper in the center of the maroon paper using gum.

2. Cut the golden tissue and paste it overlapping the golden and maroon chart paper. Keep it pressed firmly for a while.

3. Make circular coils using golden glitter on the tissue fabric. Paste the silver flowers and leaves using glue gun.

4. Stick the golden rings around the floral arrangement and also on the border of the golden chart paper.

Wedding Wishes

A simple yet attractive greeting card which would be ideal to gift to the newly wedded coupl
The embedded satin roses make this card very attractive!

You will need

Black chart paper
Silver paper 7cms X 30cms
Red satin roses
Silver tissue roses
White and red crystal stones
Water colours, silver glitter tube
Silver beads—small and big, wire
Glue gun

1. Fold the black chart paper into half. Cut the front page as shown. Stick silver paper on the inner page.

2. With the help of glue gun stick red satin roses and silver roses. Paint the other heart with red poster colour and silver colour.

3. Thread silver beads in wire and mould them in the shape of a heart. Make a smaller heart with smaller silver beads. Stick one beaded heart below the red coloured heart on the border of the silver heart.

4. Paint the border with silver colour and decorate with stones. Paste a smaller sheet inside the card to write your message.

50th Marriage Anniversary Card

When a couple celebrates 50 years of togetherness in a marriage, they have all the reasons to celebrate!

You will need

Thermocol sheet (1.5cm thickness)
Red velvet paper, white chart papers
Golden chart paper
Coloured metallic rounds
Golden pipes, golden glitter, wire
Artificial flowers, golden ribbons
Red, white stones
Soft clay, water colours
Glue gun, glue

1. Cut a thermocol sheet of size 29cms X 43cms. Cut the white chart paper of the same size and paste it on the thermocol sheet. Cut the red velvet paper of size 7.5cms X 43cms and paste it on the left side. Cut the golden chart paper of size 22cms X 27cms and paste it (refer diagram). Leave it pressed till all the layers have dried.

2. Cut the heart shape from the white chart paper and paint it with shades of red. Make candles and cake from soft clay.

3. Thread the golden beads in wire and shape like leaf and spiral coil. Cut the golden ribbons and make loops.

4. Paste the heart on the golden chart paper. Stick the wired leaves, artificial flowers, golden loops and stones.

5. Decorate with golden glitter on all the edges. Stick the cake, candles and flower arrangement below the heart. Give strokes of red paint and beautify with stones.

General Marriage Anniversary Card with Wooden Frame

This card can be made for the 1st, 25th or ev
40th marriage anniversary as the l
birds symbolise a wedded co

You will need

Thermocol sheet (1.5cm thickness)
Wooden frame coloured silver
Cream chart paper
Golden net
White frilled lace
Artificial flowers, leaves
White stones, fur, hearts of satin
Printed or painted picture of love birds
Tissue ribbons
Silver glitter, glue gun

1. Cut the thermocol sheet of size 32inch X 42inch. Make an arch (refer diagram) with a pencil and cut it with the help of a paper cutter. Paste the cream chart paper of the same size using gum and press firmly for sometime. Place the frame and mark the inner area of the wooden frame.

2. First paste the picture of the love birds and then paste the wooden frame.

3. Cut strips of 5cms X 15cms from golden net and make pleats like a fan. Tie one end with thread to give a semicircular fan shape. Make four similar fans.

4. Start arranging the flowers, leaves, white frilled lace, golden net fan and paste in an overlapping pattern. Stick the heart on the wooden frame and add the bow.

5. Cut a small piece from the cream chart paper and give it the same shape like the card. Stick the white stones on the picture and below it. Stick the small card and use it for writing the anniversary wishes. Decorate with silver glitter.

Greeting Card with Punching Flowers

Artificial flowers can be replaced with punching flowers. This is a simple floral card where the clay motifs can be changed according to the occasion.

You will need

White chart paper
Mustard yellow, beige chart paper
Art paper sheets (Cream, yellow, mustard, brown)
Green art paper for leaves
M seal (White), talcum powder
Gum, pearls
Water colours, golden glitter
Punches of different shapes of flowers and leaves

1. Punch flowers of different shapes from the cream, yellow, mustard and brown art papers. Punch the leaves from green art paper. Using talcum powder on your hands mix the M seal. Mould it like two abstract figures and paint.

2. Cut the white chart paper of size 25cms X 36cms and fold in half. Cut 'L' shape of 5cms thickness from mustard chart paper and paste on the card. Cut three strips of size 10cms X 2cms from the beige chart paper and paste (refer diagram) using gum.

3. Stick all the paper flowers and green leaves overlapping each other. Use the small flowers on top of the bigger flower.

4. Paste M seal motifs in the centre. Decorate with golden glitter. Using white paint make curls around the floral arrangements.

25th Marriage Anniversary Card

An elegant 25th anniversary card with silver sparrows to celebrate the silver jubilee.

You will need

Thermocol sheet size 28cms X 40cms (1.5mm thickness)
Red, black, silver chart paper
M-seal, talcum powder
One artificial sparrow
White stones flowers
Red stones small and big
Green crystal leaves
Silver fabric colour, silver ribbon
Silver glitter, silver thread

1. Cut the thermocol sheet of size 28cms X 40cms. Cut the red chart paper of same size and paste it on the thermocol sheet. Cut the grey sheet of size 24cms X 10cms and the black chart paper of size 20cms X 23cms and paste (refer diagram). Let the layers dry completely.

2. Mix the M seal using talcum powder on your hands. Roll into thin pipes and twist two pipes and form a branch. Make several branches. Paste the black chart paper using glue. Cut the plastic sparrow into half in such a way that you get two half sparrow bodies. Paste on the black chart paper and balance with more M seal branches.

3. Stick the stone flowers, red stones and leaves. Paint the branches and sparrows silver. Also paint a few silver branches.

4. Paste the silver ribbons. Make a ribbon flower at the right corner. Beautify with red stones and silver glitter.

Variation: You can mold the sparrows out of clay also.

Traditional Greeting Card

A bejewelled stone border on a miniature painting is the beauty of this card. It can be used for a wedding anniversary or a wedding invitation also.

You will need

Soft wood or ply wood
White textured paper
Cut-out of a miniature painting
Green, red, golden textured paper
White stones—round and drop shaped
Red stones, green stones
Feather, toothpick
Golden glitter, golden string

1. Take a softwood of size 13cms X 20cms. Cut the white textured paper of the same size and paste on it. Cut the miniature painting in a round shape with diameter 12cms. Cut two mango-like shape from the golden chart paper and paste. (Refer template)

2. Cut the green chart paper. Crease and fold (refer diagram) to form a small card. Paste the feather and stones on the card. Make two holes and put golden strings. Paste a red paper strip on the right flap.

3. Paste the small green card overlapping the miniature painting. For making the stone border first stick the red stones at equal distance. Make the stone flower with the white drop-shaped stones around the red stones. Now stick the white stones line-wise and make the whole border.

4. Stick the green stones in the centre of the mango shaped golden chart paper. Stick drop-shaped white stones around it. Stick the green stones and the white stones on the left side of the card also.

5. Paste the red paper on two sides of the green card. Make thin lines with golden glitter. Give border to the stone work with golden glitter. Paste the feather and stones on the right corner also.

Variation: You may use the miniature cut-out from a used wedding card or calender.

General Floral Card on Framed Glass

This card can be used for any occasion like marriage anniversary, birthday or house warming. The black frame on the glass makes this card ideal for the shelf.

You will need

A glass with black frame
Cream chart paper, printed or painted floral picture
Acrylic sheet size 32cms X 20cms
Artificial flowers
Pearls, stones, hearts of satin or fur
Tissue ribbon, 3 big buttons
Jute sheet
Lace of pearls, silver glitter
Glue gun, gum

1. Take a glass of size 38cms X 30cms and get it framed with a black border. Cut the floral picture of size 23cms X 16cms and paste it on the left corner of the glass. Cut the jute strip of size 8cms X 30cms and paste it on the glass.

2. Cut the cream chart paper of size 14cms X 19 cms and write the text. Paste it overlapping the corner of the floral picture. Stick the hearts, artificial flowers and stones on the edges.

3. Stick the three big buttons using glue gun on the floral picture. Balance the acrylic sheet on the three buttons and stick it using glue gun.

4. Stick the bow, pearls and artificial flowers on the acrylic sheet. Decorate with silver glitter and pearl borders.

Birthday Card Using Net Fabric

The fancy woven net fabric highlights this card, which is ideal for the cute Birthday girl!

You will need

Chart paper (Peach colour)
Thermocol
Net fabric, Satin ribbon
Doll motif
Artificial flowers, leaves
Silver glitter
Poster colour
Gum, glue gun

1. Fold the peach chart paper into half. Paint red poster colour from the top and give shading till the bottom. Cut a small piece from the thermocol as shown in the diagram. Paste a coloured sheet on the top and paste this piece in the centre of the card.

2. Cut a long strip from the net of size 7cms X 40cms. Giving a pleated effect paste the net using glue gun.

3. Give finishing to the border by pasting satin ribbon. Stick artificial flowers, leaves, roses and make a border. Stick the doll motif on the thermocol piece.

4. Decorate the corners with silver glitter, sequins lace and butterflies.

Variation: You may also put the child's photo in place of the motif.

New Born Baby Girl Greeting Card

A baby girl is one of the most beautiful miracles in life!
Making a card for the arrival of the little one has always been fun.

You will need

Thermocol sheet 30cms X 35cms (1cm thick)
White and pink chart paper
Soft toy of baby girl or any toy
White lacy frill
Artificial flowers
Stones, sticker
Poster colour—Pink
Satin ribbons, glue gun

1. Cut the thermocol sheet very neatly. Cut another window in this rectangle of size 7cms X 14cms. Paste a pink chart paper on the thermocol sheet after cutting the window portion.

2. Knead two different coloured clay and roll into thin pipes. Shape the pipes as shown and let them dry.

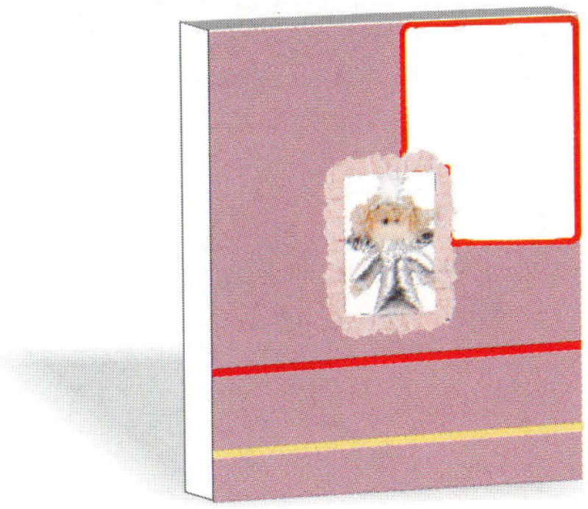

3. Paste the white chart paper on the top right corner. With the help of glue gun stick the soft toy. Stick the pink and yellow satin ribbons at the bottom. Stick the white lacy frill on the border of the window.

4. Stick the clay shapes and a ribbon bow on the top. Make a decorative border using stickers, stones and flowers. Use the same white frill on the borders of the thermocol sheet.

Variation: You may also use a small teddy bear in place of the puppet.

3D Card for Baby Boy

This is an easy card which gives a three dimensional effect for a newly born baby boy!

You will need

A coloured picture of a baby boy
Chart papers of three shades of blue
Water colours
Double sided foam tape
Small plastic butterflies

1. Cut 2 pieces of flower from the light blue chart paper and 3 pieces of flowers from the dark blue chart paper. Get 3 coloured photocopies of the baby picture and cut along the boundaries.

2. Fold a chart paper like a card and stick the chart paper flowers overlapping each other with the help of double tape.

3. Paste all the 3 coloured photocopy pictures using double tape on all the 3 layers to give a 3 dimensional effect. For a neat look stick small pieces of double tape behind every picture.

4. Using water colours paint the grass, flowers and the initials on the flowers. Decorate with butterflies.

House Warming Greeting Card

'Home sweet home' is what every family feels when they build their new house. So greet them with this handmade card when they throw a house warming party!

You will need

White chart paper
Artificial satin roses
Green chart paper
Water colours
Ribbon for bow
Glue, glue gun

1. Fold a white chart paper into half. First sketch the house and using water colours paint the house giving a shaded effect. Paint the grass using yellow and green shades of water colour.

2. Take the green chart paper and cut like grass (refer template) and paste below the painted house.

3. Stick the satin roses using glue gun.

4. Make a bow and stick on the painted pillar.

Variation: You may use a printed picture of a house from a magazine.

For My School Greeting Card

This is a greeting card which may be given on 'Teacher's day' or to your school faculty when you get a farewell party!

You will need

White chart paper
Blue printed paper
Thermocol sheet (1cm thickness)
Water colours
Black soft clay
Black, blue satin ribbon
Floral leather lace
Silver glitter, white stones

1. Fold a white chart paper into half. Paste the blue chart paper on the lower half of the card.

2. Cut a thermocol sheet of size 20cms X 10cms. and stick a white chart paper of the same size. Sketch the scenery and paint with water colours. Make the graduation cap, question mark and number tag with the black clay. Leave to dry.

3. Paste the thermocol sheet in the centre of the card. Stick black satin ribbon on the sides of the thermocol sheet and also on the left corner. Make a bow of blue satin ribbon and paste on the black strips.

4. Paste the clay motifs. Paste the floral lace in the lower part of the card.

Variation: You may put your school group photo also.

Bags for All Seasons!

Making Gift Bags

It is always good to give gifts in paper gift bags which are decorated. Making the right size of bag for your gift makes it more personalized. You can buy bright coloured sheets of different textures and keep plain bags ready for decorating. The ideas in this book will inspire you to make fancy decorative bags according to your taste and ability. Start with simple ideas and very soon you will know how to use every bit of decoration lying around your home. So this season give meaningful gifts in beautiful bags to your loved ones!

Basic Bag

Basic Paper Bag Folding

For making a paper bag you need a chart paper, or a thick paper, so that the bag can hold the gift Items. The measurement and the creasing are very important for a neat bag.
You can increase the size of the bag as per your requirement by referring this basic method

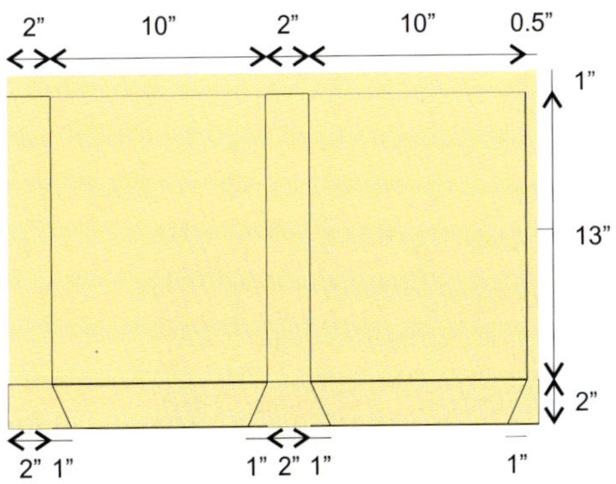

1. Take a thick paper of size 24.5 inch x 16 inch. Draw all the lines as shown in diagram(1) using a pencil on the inner side of the paper

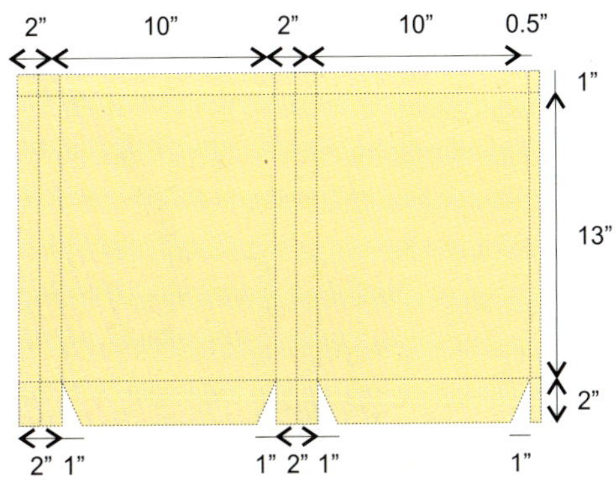

2. Cut the 1 inch triangles and crease all the lines using a butter knife or any pointed object

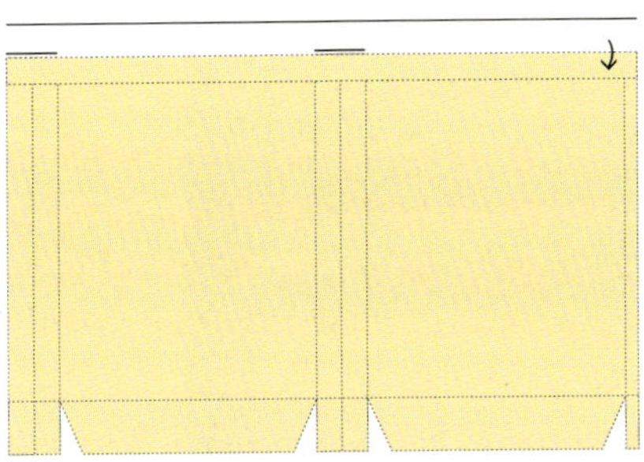

3. Fold and paste the 1 inch strip Shown at the top of the bag

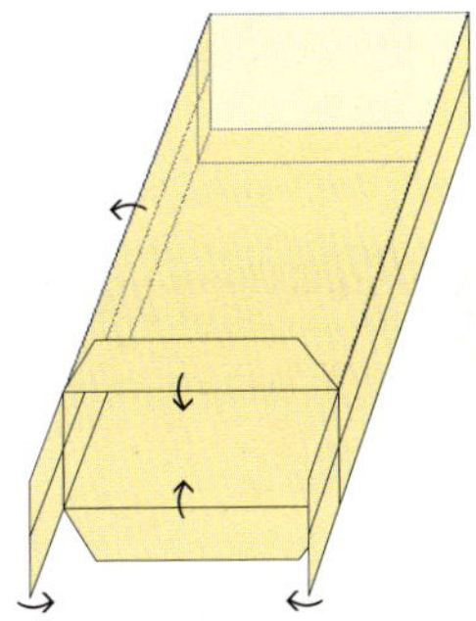

4. Now complete the folds of the bag and paste the base of the bag using glue

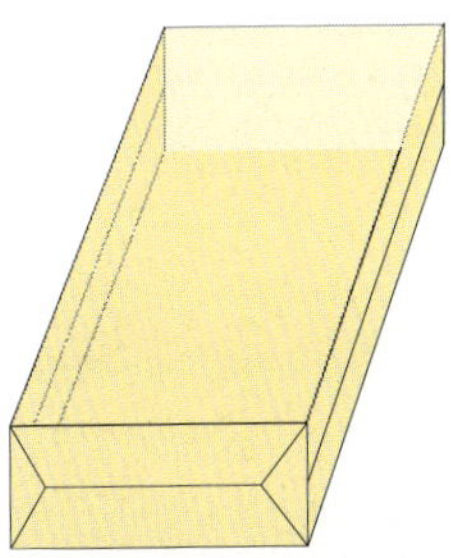

5. Press all the folds again and complete the bag

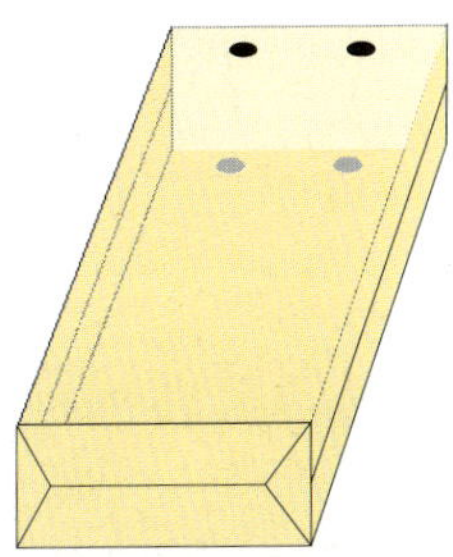

6. Make two holes and put the strings. Tie knots in the inner side of the bag

Gift Bag Using Silver Golden Ribbons

This is a very simple yet elegant paper bag which requires very little time and material. Ideally useful for decorating bags in large quantity.

You will need

A paper bag
Silver-Golden ribbons
White stones
Silver glitter tube
Golden rings
Glue gun

1. Cut two strips from a broad golden ribbon. Using gum, paste the golden strips starting from the edge of the bag till the centre. Similarly stick the silver strips.

2. Tie a knot using all the ends of the strips. Trim the ends to get equal length.

3. Decorate with golden rings, stones and silver glitter. You can attach a tag of a similar design as shown in the picture.

Gift Bag Using Coloured Paper Sheets

You will need

A paper bag
Coloured chart paper
Black satin ribbon
Textured wrapping paper
Silver glitter
Glue

1. Cut 5 strips of thickness 5 cm, 4 cm, 3 cm, 2 cm,1 cm respectively from different coloured chart papers. Paste all the strips at equal distance.

2. Paste satin ribbon on these strips using glue gun.

3. Cut petals from the textured wrapping paper. Stick 3 petals to form a flower.

4. Decorate with silver glitter.

Gift Bag Using Thermocol Balls and Fur

You will need

Paper bag
Thermocol balls
Fur
Silver and Pink satin ribbons
White stones
Thermocol sheet of 10mm thickness
Silver glitter tube, Poster colours
Gum, glue gun, thermocol cutter

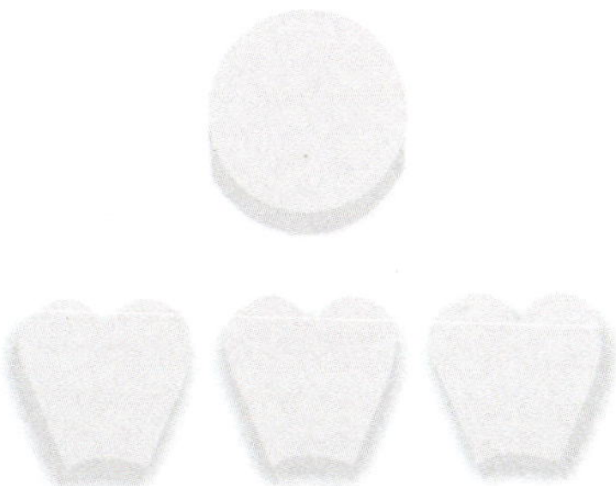

1. Cut one circle and three heart shaped pieces from a thermocol sheet.

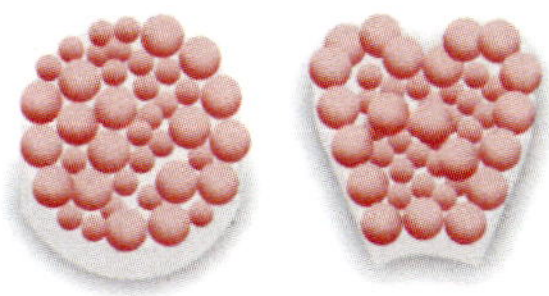

2. Paste thermocol balls on all the pieces using glue, taking care not to leave any empty space. Colour all the pieces giving a shaded look.

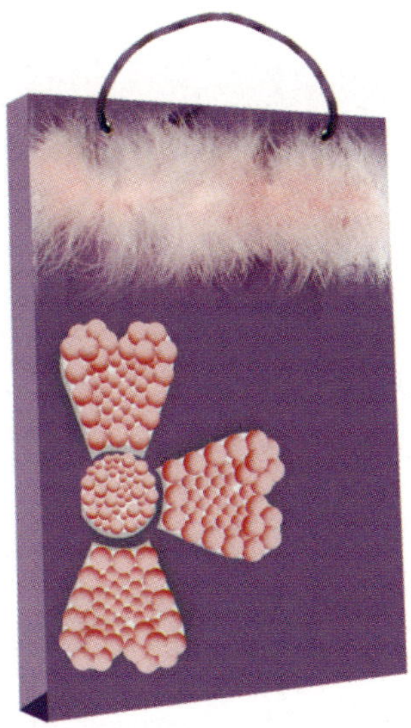

3. Paste the satin ribbons and then paste the fur and thermocol pieces using glue gun.

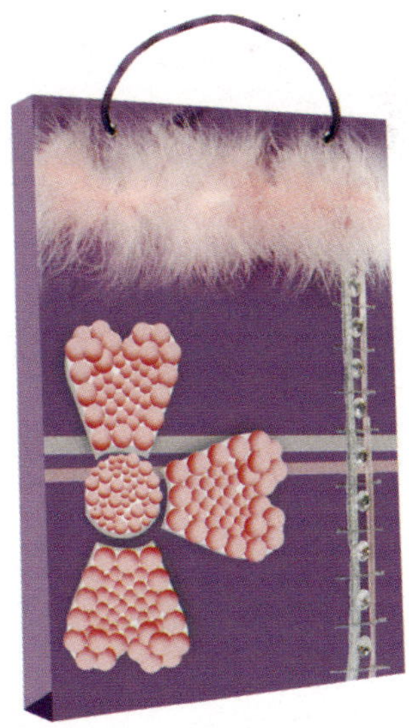

4. Decorate using satin ribbons, sliver ribbons, white stones and silver glitter.

Gift Bag Using butter paper

You will need

A paper bag
Butter paper sheet
Printed paper
White stones
Sequins lace
Satin ribbons
Artificial flowers
Glue gun
Silver glitter tube

1. Cut a printed paper of size 13X14cms
   Paste it in the lower centre of the bag

2. Cut the butter paper sheet as shown in the diagram (2) and fold it in a pleated form giving the shape of a flower pot. Similarly fold a rectangular piece in a pleated form.

3. Paste the pleated flower pot and rectangular butter paper using a glue gun. Use white satin ribbon to make branches in the flower pot. Make bow and stick on the rectangle. Stick the same ribbon in the centre of the bag overlapping the pot and in the corner of the bag.

4. Use two flowers for the pot and decorate with silver glitter. Stick the sequins lace and stones to complete the bag.

Gift Bag Using Paper Roses

You will need

A paper bag
Yellow and White chart paper
Pearls
Yellow satin ribbons
Silver ribbons
Silver metal leaves
Glue gun
Silver glitter tube

1. Cut a circle of diameter 8cm from a yellow chart paper. Starting from the edge cut the circle in a strip form till the centre.

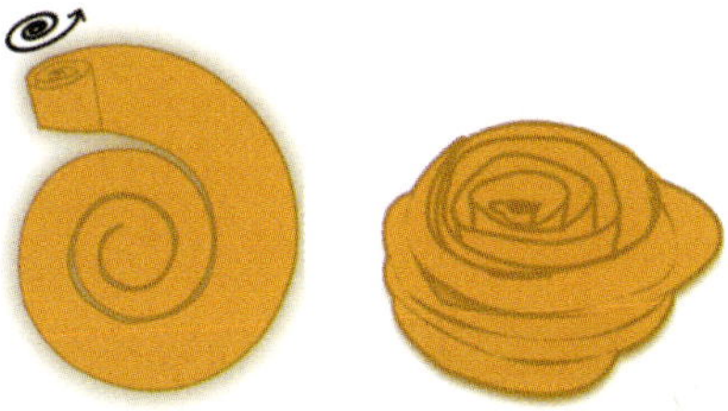

2. Roll the strip using your fingers towards the centre. Paste the rose with the base of the circle. Similarly make roses as needed.

3. Stick the yellow satin ribbons diagonally at equal distance. Arrange and paste all paper roses and pearls.

4. Decorate the bag with silver leaves and silver glitter. You can make a bunch of loops of silver and yellow ribbons and tie with the handle.

Gift Bag with metallic hearts

You will need

A paper bag
Red, pink satin ribbons
Glitter powder-red, pink
Red sparkle tube
White chart paper
Silver, pink glitter tube
Silver chart paper
Glue gun
Double sided foam tape

1. Cut different sizes of strips from red and pink satin ribbons. Paste the ribbons horizontally leaving equal space between the ribbons.

2. Cut hearts from white chart paper. Spread glue and sprinkle glitter powder on all hearts. Leave to dry. Stick the hearts according to the arrangement.

3. Using double sided foam tape stick the smaller hearts made of silver chart paper.

4. Make a zig-zag pattern using pink glitter tube.

Gift Bag Using Clay

The clay motifs can be changed along with the shades of the papers and used for any occasion. For example for marriage anniversary the motifs can be made of two hearts with the shades of red as background.

You will need

Chart paper of 4 different blue shades
White chart paper, butter paper
A paper bag
Soft clay
Satin flowers and lace
Silver sequins, silver glitter tube
Glue gun

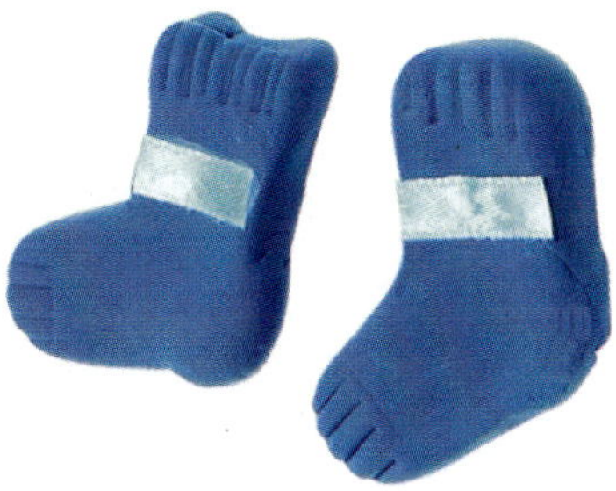

1. Using soft clay make a pair of socks. With a paper knife give texture of lines and stick a blue ribbon on it.

2. Tear strips from four shades of blue chart paper with hand to give it an unfinished edge. Stick the strips at equal distance.

3. Cut an oval shape from white chart paper and paste it in the center of the bag. Paste a bigger oval shaped butter paper overlapping the white oval.

4. Paste the pair of socks, flowers and a bow made from ribbons. Highlight with silver sequins and glitter.

Paper bags for a gift hamper

Any occasion can be made special if it is pre-planned with gifts which are wrapped and given in paper bags of a similar colour theme!

You will need

Bags of 4 sizes
Yellow, Orange chart paper
Corrugated sheet, OHP sheet
Golden, Silver ribbons
White stones
Golden sequins
Silver glitter tube, glue
Artificial flowers, glue gun

1. Apply glue on the paper bag and sprinkle golden sequins. Remove extra sequins by inverting the bag.

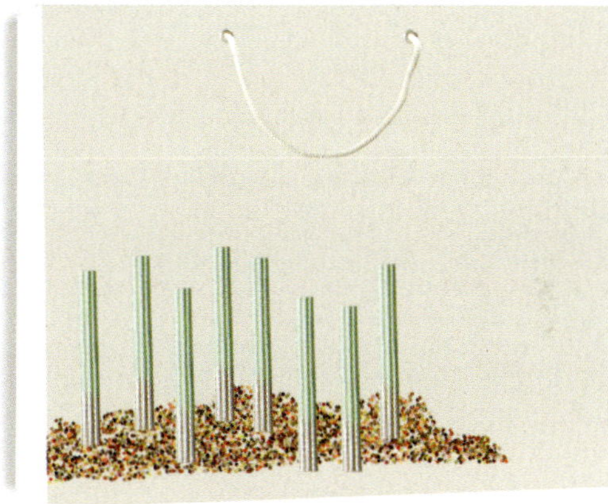

2. Cut pieces of size 11cms x 8cms from the corrugated sheet. Roll each piece to form a pipe. Paste the edge stick of all the pipes at equal distance.

3. Cut drop shaped petals from orange chart paper and smaller drops from yellow chart paper. Paste both the coloured pieces overlapping each other.

4. Stick golden and silver bows and decorate the candle glow with silver glitter tube and white stones.

Bag for gifting accessories!

You will need

Paper bag
Yellow, Orange chart paper
Corrugated sheet, OHP sheet
Golden, Silver ribbons
White stones
Golden sequins
Silver glitter tube, glue
Artificial flowers, glue gun

1. For this bag you will need a medium sized paper bag. Refer basic paper bag folding method and reduce the measurements according to your requirements.

2. From the corrugated sheet cut two similar pieces as shown in the diagram (Refer template) and paste on both the sides of the bag.

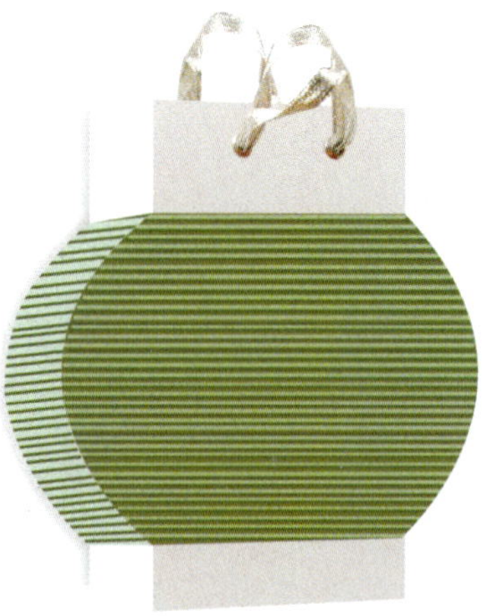

3. Measure the width of the bag. Using this measurement cut two strips from the corrugated sheet. Paste the strips on the curved edges on both the side.

4. Decorate with artificial flower, golden bow, orange and yellow strips and silver glitter.

Bag for gifting Vase, candles!

You will need

Paper bag
Yellow, Orange chart paper
Corrugated sheet, OHP sheet
Golden, Silver ribbons
White stones
Golden sequins
Silver glitter tube, glue
Artificial flowers, glue gun

1. Make a tall paper bag of size 16cms X 21cms by referring basic paper bag folding method.

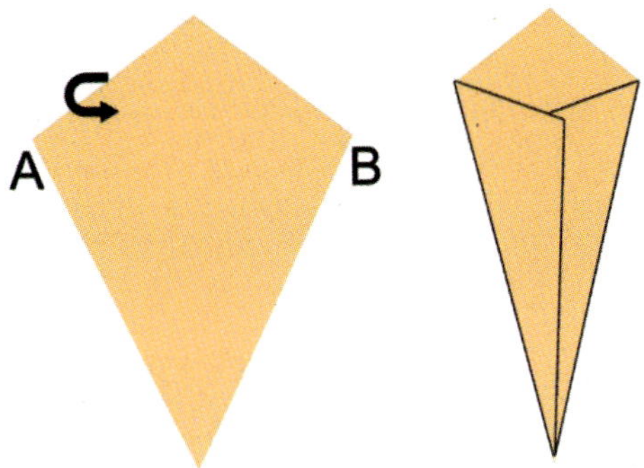

2. Cut diamond shaped pieces from the yellow and orange chart paper. Fold both A and B towards the centre. Paste the flaps and make a petal. Make eight similar petals for one flower.

3. Stick the petals like a flower with a stone in the centre.

4. Decorate with corrugated pieces, ribbons and a golden bow.

Bag for Chocolates

You will need

Bags of 4 sizes
Yellow, Orange chart paper
Corrugated sheet, OHP sheet
Golden, Silver ribbons
White stones
Golden sequins
Silver glitter tube, glue
Artificial flowers, glue gun

1. Before pasting the basic small paper bag cut a window of size 6cms X 4cms from the front side. Cut a bigger size OHP sheet and paste on the window. Now fold and paste the basic paper bag.

2. Paste silver ribbon on the window frame. Stick yellow, orange and corrugated strips at equal distance.

3. Decorate with golden bow, golden sequins and stones.

How to reuse Paper Shopping Bags

More and more stores are providing paper bags to help the environment. Reusing these paper shopping bags as gift bags is very economical and less time consuming. So the next time you go shopping and get a paper bag start collecting them and decorate with these simple ideas!

Reusing a paper bag with Golden paint and coconut thread

A printed brown paper bag can be redecorated and used as a gift bag!

You will need

A small brown paper bag
Golden paint
Coconut thread
Gum

1. Paint golden colour on all the printed areas of the bag

2. Stick the coconut thread in a zig-zag pattern

Reusing a Paper bag fo Children's Gifts

Small presents can be gifted in these bags. You can make these bags and keep them fo those hectic days when you are short of time

You will need

Black chart paper
Golden paint
Few fresh leaves
Golden ribbons
Golden glitter tube

1. Cut two rectangular pieces from a black chart paper and paste them on the printed areas of the bag.

2. Dip a leaf in golden paint and stamp on the bag carefully. Similarly repeat all over the bag. Take care not to use too much of paint so as to get the dry effect.

3. Make a golden bow and paste it in the centre. Paste a golden ribbon at the bottom also.

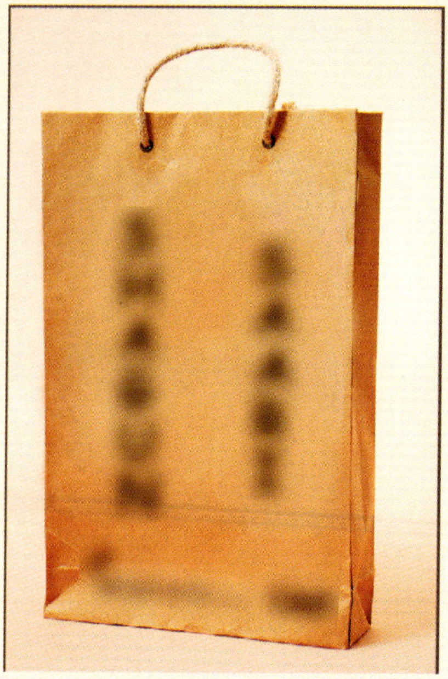

Reusing a bag with Leaf printing

If bigger areas are to be covered it's better to paste a new paper on the printed areas.

You will need

Black chart paper
Golden paint
Few fresh leaves
Golden ribbons
Golden glitter tube

1. Cut two rectangular pieces from a black chart paper and paste them on the printed areas of the bag.

2. Dip a leaf in golden paint and stamp on the bag carefully. Similarly repeat all over the bag. Take care not to use too much of paint so as to get the dry effect.

3. Make a golden bow and paste it in the centre. Paste a golden ribbon at the bottom also.

Reusing a paper bag with wrapping papers

This bag takes minimum time and material. I have used only bits of wrapping papers to cover the printed areas. So before you make a bag keep in mind the printed areas which should be covered neatly.

You will need

Different types of printed papers
Gum

1. Cut different sizes of rectangles from various printed wrapping papers. Stick them overlapping each other.

Variation: you can also stick a satin ribbon bow or artificial flowers on one corner of the bag.

Reusing a bag for a Birthday Party

This is a simple bag which you can make with your kids. Bright coloured papers have been used to make it attractive for a birthday party.

You will need

Various coloured chart papers
Plastic straws
Coloured pens
Silver glitter
Satin ribbons
Glue

1. Cut oval shaped coloured papers and stick on the printed areas overlapping a bit.

2. Cut plastic straws of one inch and paste at the bottom of the bag. Do not leave any space between the pipes.

3. Write 'Happy Birthday' with coloured pens. Decorate with silver glitter and satin ribbons.

25th Marriage Anniversary Greeting Card with Paper Bag!

A 25th anniversary is a wonderful opportunity to give something handmade and meaningful. So express your feelings that you admire their relationship and hope they have a happy life togeth that lasts eternally.

You will need

Black or white chart paper
Soft red clay
Crushed tissue fabric
Wire
Beads and silver pipes
Silver laces and zig-zag
Silver sequins
Silver glitter tube, silver paint
Glue gun

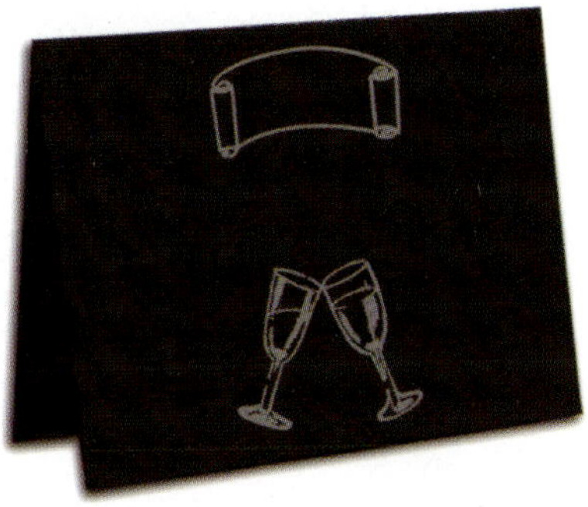

1. Fold the black chart paper horizontally. Paint the glass and the arched box with silver colour.

2. Thread one bead and one pipe alternately in wire. Shape it like a leaf.

3. Stick this beaded wire on the crushed tissue fabric. Trim like a leaf. Make similar eight leaves.

4. Roll the soft clay into pipes using palm. Shape it in digits of 2 and 5.

5. Paste the 25 in the silver arched box. Give shape of a heart near the glasses drawn.

6. Arrange the leaves, lace, clay pipes, a few stones, sequins at the two top corners of the card. Decorate with silver sequins and silver glitter.

7. Make a small chocolate paper bag and decorate it using laces and sequins lace.

8. For the tag—draw two small glasses. Decorate with silver glitter tube and flowers.

Variation: You can gift this hamper in a cane basket with your gift and flowers.

Making Hampers

Making your own gift basket is a wonderful way of presenting small gifts in a decorative way. You can personalise the gift basket according to the occasion or the couple to whom you are gifting. Expensive gifts when placed on a decorated tray can be highlighted beautifully.

In this chapter I have shown how to decorate various types of baskets according to the theme of the occasion. You can be as simple or elaborate as you want to be. You can also prepare a complete gift hamper if you want to give more gifts and make the occasion special. So make these beautiful and unique hampers which will be useful and remembered for years to come.

Gift Hamper for Baby Boy

Welcome the newborn baby boy with this beautiful basket filled with his toys and accessories. Gift the card along with the basket and express your joy for the family.

You will need

For the Card
White chart paper 56cms X 36cms
Shades of blue chart paper
Lace, silver ribbons
Blue chart paper
Small motifs of teddy, bow
Artificial flowers
Poster colours
Silver glitter, glue

For the Basket
One oval shaped cane basket,
Plastic straws
Thermocol 5cm thick
Glue gun
Water colours
Blue satin fabric
White frilled lace

1. Fold the white chart paper into half. Cut nine rectangles of size 10cms X 7cms from all the three shades of blue chart paper. Leave 5cms space from the bottom and paste all the nine rectangles at equal distance.

2. Cut the Boy initials from the dark blue chart paper and paste on the rectangles of the middle line.

3. Paste the silver ribbons and overlap with blue satin ribbons

4. Stick the artificial flowers, bows and teddy motifs (you can use any small decorative accessories for this). Give outlines with silver glitter to finish the card.

For the Basket

1. Cut 6 cubes of 5cms X 5cms from the thermocol sheet using a cutter.

2. Paint them in shades of blue and paste one alphabet on each side.

3. Cut balloon shape from blue chart paper and outline with silver glitter. Paste the balloon on the plastic straw. Similarly paste artificial flowers on the plastic straw.

4. Cover the basket with satin cloth using glue gun at the edges. Arrange the cubes and paste them one over the other. Stick all the other decoration.

For the Bag

1. Cut the rattle from white chart paper and paint it with water colour.

3. Paste the blue satin ribbon and the artificial flower. Put double sided tape behind the rattle and stick on the bag. Decorate with a bow. Paste the stones and complete the bag.

Wedding Hamper for Gifts

This is a simple yet elegant tray to present expensive gifts on a wedding ceremony. The pearl border expresses how precious the wedding is for you.

You will need

Thermocol 3cms thickness
Big pearls
Red satin ribbons
Red, White plastic ribbons
Mirror based tray or any flat tra
Glue gun
Silver paint

1. According to the size of your tray cut two right angle shapes from the thermocol sheet. Colour with silver paint. Wrap the red satin ribbon leaving equal gap and paste the end of the ribbon.

2. Cut strips of 18cms from the red and white plastic ribbons. Make loops from all the strips and staple the ends. Arrange all the loops and tie in a bunch.

3. Paste the right angled thermocol borders on the opposite corners.

4. Using glue gun paste the pearls overlapping each other and make a border. Stick the ribbon bunch on one corner. Curl the red and white ribbon together and paste near the bunch.

Wedding Chocolate Basket

A chocolate basket with a bouquet of hearts is a perfect gift for special occasions if you have a limited budget. The handmade bouquet shows your thoughtfulness along with a personalised touch.

You will need

A cane basket
Thermocol sheet (1cm thickness)
Pencils - 10 pieces
Silver paint
Sequins, stones, pearls, pipes, white satin roses
Red, blue, silver satin ribbons
Blue, White net
White frill lace
Glue gun, glue, cutter

1. From the thermocol sheet cut ten hearts of same size using a cutter. Apply glue on heart and stick stones closely. Take care not to leave any space between the stones. Similarly, stick the sequins, pearls, pipes, roses on the other heart and paste the silver ribbon on the sides of all hearts.

2. Sharpen the pencils from both sides and paint with silver colour. Apply glue on one end of the pencil and insert into one heart. Tie red satin ribbon at the joint. Similarly make other heart sticks.

3. Cut five square pieces of thermocol of size 10cms X 10cms and paste them together. Insert heart sticks in the thermocol base.

4. Cut two big squares from the white and blue net so as to cover the thermocol base. Tie thread after collecting the net from all sides in the centre. Trim the net so as to give a frilled look.

5. Paste the heart bouquet on one corner of the basket. Stick white frill lace on the edge of the basket using glue gun. Tie two hearts together and paste on one corner.

Gift Hamper for Baby Girl

This is a complete gift hamper with a wide assortment of gifts for a baby girl. Fill it with goodies and make the new mom and dad completely delighted as they receive it.

You will need

For cane basket
Tissue fabric - Pink, peach, silver
Net fabric - Pink, purple
Ribbons - Pink, silver
Chart papers - White, pink, purple
Colourful thermocol balls
Thin wire, wire cutter
White stones (big)
Silver glitter
thermocol sheet - 5cms thickness
pencil

For chocolate board
Artificial flowers
cardboard 22cms X 30cms
Wrapping paper
Chocolate balls
String

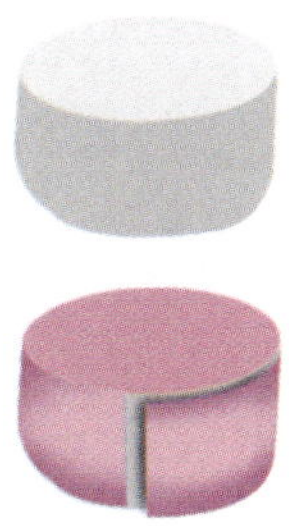

1. Cut a circle form the thermocol sheet of diameter 10cms. Cut a strip of purple chart paper and paste around the thermocol base. Also paste a purple circle on the top.

2. Cut the dress from white chart paper (refer template); cut only the dress from the peach chart paper (refer template).

3. Stick a pencil behind the paper dress. Decorate the dress with small roses and silver glitter.

4. Paste net behind the paper frock. Stick stones and pink satin ribbon on the purple base.

5. Cut a strip of 10cms X 5cms from the pink tissue fabric. Fold the edges of the tissue inside. Fold it in half and tie the ends with a thread. Similarly make tissue petals of pink, peach and silver tissue fabric according to the size of your basket.

6. Cut the wire of size 21cms and a smaller wire of size 17cms. Thread with coloured thermocol balls and twist the end to form a loop. Similarly make the smaller loop and join both the loops.

7. Paste all the tissue petals overlapping each other and form half of the border of the basket. Tie the pink and purple net together at equal distance using pink satin ribbon. Paste on the other half border of the basket.

8. Paste the thermocol ball loops and the paper frock stand. Make a bunch of loops from the silver ribbon and stick on one corner. Make a bow from silver satin ribbon and paste over it.

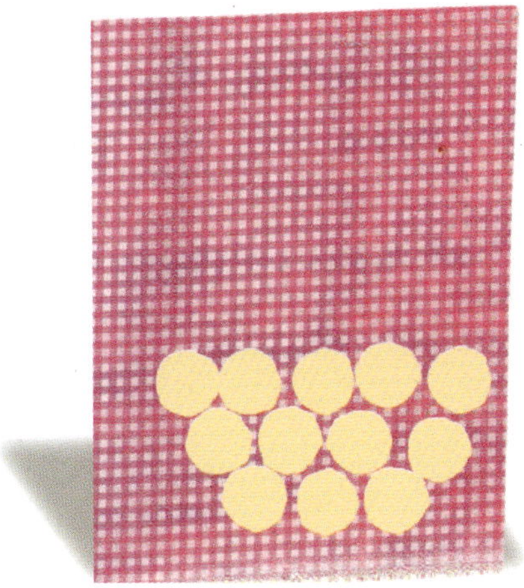

9. Wrap a cardboard with a bright wrapping paper. Paste the chocolate balls in the shape of a pot.

10. Paste the artificial flowers and string. Wrap the satin ribbon as boundary for the chocolate balls.

11. Make the card using the same paper frock motif. Make a butterfly using two tissue petals and paste on the corner of the card. Paste thermocol balls for the body of the butterfly. Decorate with stones and silver glitter.

Diwali Hamper

A tray of dry fruits can be the best form of diwali gift from your side to your near and dear ones for making their diwali special. Lord Ganesha with the traditional umbrella brings out the importance of this festival.

You will need

A flat cane basket
A small basket for traditional umbrella
Chart papers - light green, dark green, white
Printed or plain red fabric
Artificial plastic leaves
Golden glitter powder, golden paint, silver powder
Red stones, red lace
Mirrors, shells
Golden, silver ribbons
Glue, glue gun
Pencil
Idol of Lord Ganesh
Small thermocol piece

1. Take a small cane basket and cover with the red fabric using glue gun. Paste the edges on the top of the basket. Paste the lower edges of the fabric inside the basket.

2. Decorate the basket with mirrors, shells and red stones. Complete the edge of the basket with a beaded lace.

3. Paint the pencil with golden colour. Stick the umbrella on one end of the pencil using glue gun. Insert the other end in the thermocol piece.

4. Cut 4 petals each from the light green and dark green chart papers. The number of petals depends on the size of your basket.

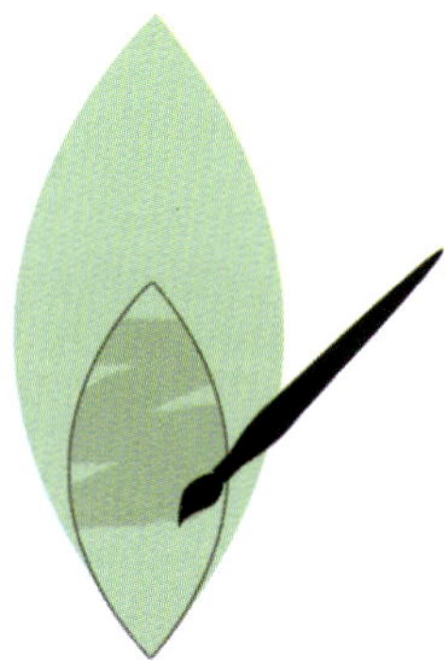

5. Apply glue with a paint brush in the shape of a smaller petal (refer diagram) Dip it in golden powder. Tap the petal and remove the extra golden powder. Let the leaves dry completely.

6. Make dark green petals using silver powder and light green petals using golden powder.

7. Similarly apply glue on the plastic leaves and dip in golden and silver powder. Let the leaves dry completely.

8. Paint the cane basket with golden paint. Leave to dry.

9. Stick the umbrella with the thermocol base on the edge of the cane basket. Stick the Ganesh idol.

10. Paste the paper leaves and plastic leaves alternately and make a border. Decorate with shells and stones.

11. Paste a golden and silver bow in the center. Divide the basket into sections using strips of white chart paper.

Birthday Wishes

Hope every single minutes of your day
Will hold in store
All the special birthday fun
That you've been waiting for.

May your birthday blossom into a beautiful year
Filled with surprise and happiness.

As your birthday is here
Let the celebration start
Enjoy life's precious gifts
And always remain young at heart.

Wishing you all the things
That bring beauty to your world
And joy to your heart;
The special things that give you
Happy moments today
And happy memories tomorrow.

Wedding Wishes

The special joys of sharing life together
May these be yours today and forever
For when two people believe that love's forever
It shows in the life they've created together.

Anniversary Wishes

May every moment that you share
Of dreams that you have seen come true,
Help make this special day
A happy one for you.

Wishing that the little world you have created together
Be a paradise of love.

New born Baby Boy

These golden days of childhood come and go very fast,
So hold him tight and love him dearly,
And make these precious moments last.

BOY

It's time to change the nappies
To cuddle your little one
To be with him every time
To nurture your most beautiful dream
Wishing you best for him always.

New born Baby Boy

A baby girl ... one of the most beautiful miracles in life
One of the greatest joys we can ever know
And one of the reasons why
There is extra sunshine, laughter and happiness
In your world today.

All the best

It's time to put in your best
To prove yourself and come out with flying colours
Here's hoping that whatever you wish
Would be yours with success–Good luck for everything.

Basic craft tools

It is always convenient to start a craft project if you keep a craft tool box ready with some of these basic tools.

Ruler

Use a 12" metal ruler when you use a craft knife to cut against the edge. You should also have a transparent plastic ruler to mark lines while seeing the image.

Scissors

A few pairs of large and small scissors are a necessity for all the cutting work. Use the large scissors for heavy material and thick paper sheets. The small scissors can be used for cutting around edges and snipping out small shapes.

Paper cutter

It is useful for cutting perfectly straight lines.
The bigger cutters are used for thermocol cutting and the smaller ones are useful for paper.

Glue

Glue is a must in a craft kit.
Paper sticking should be done using glue as it dries easily and has a strong bond.

Glue gun

It is an electric tool used after heating for applying adhesive.
The adhesive is available in the form of solid sticks of glue.
Once applied these adhesives are very strong and suitable for bonding heavy objects.

Craft punches

These stamp out a shaped hole in paper.
Craft stores offer a wide variety of punches of different shapes, sizes and motifs.

Rivet punch

This punch is used for making holes in paper bags and to attach the aluminium ring around the punched hole.

Tape

A roll of transparent tape with a dispenser is useful for wrapping gifts.

Double sided tape

This tape has adhesive on both sides and is useful to stick paper overlaps so that they stay invisible.

Brushes

Keep several brushes of different sizes for painting. It is best to keep a few brushes that are fine, some medium and a few broad brushes.

50

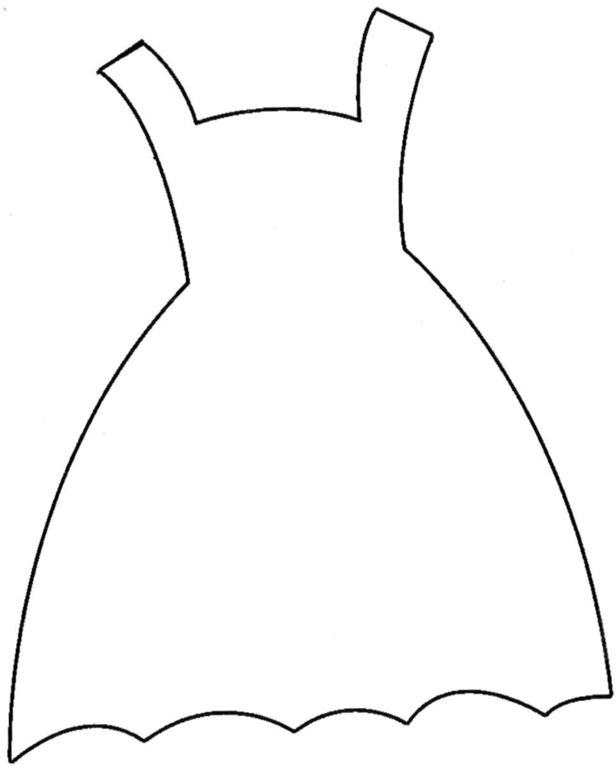